Teaching Mathematics with the Internet

by Marc Alan Rosner

David Kershaw, Contributing Writer
Todd Frey, Editor
Kathleen Housley, Senior Editor

Companion Web Site

This book has a companion Web site at http://twi.classroom.com/math/712/

There are no URL addresses in this book. Each lesson plan has numbered Web sites that correspond to the URLs listed at the companion Web site. For example, a lesson plan called "Lesson Sample" would have three Web sites listed in the book: labeled:  1, 2, and 3. On the companion Web site, you would find "Lesson Sample" and the three numbered Web sites listed below the title.

URL addresses are checked weekly by our chief cybrarian. However, sometimes Web sites disappear from the Internet completely. In that case, a new comparable site may replace the original. On some occasions, the site is rearranged and reflowed, so our lesson plans may not follow the order/content of the featured Web site. For these reasons, it's wise to always visit the featured Web sites before you send yo

---

ABOUT THE AUTHOR

Marc Rosner is a teacher in New York State with 10 years' experience in the classroom. He is also an educational consultant and writer, specializing in computing and technology. His work has appeared in diverse publications including The Science Teacher, Scientific American Frontiers, Gannett Suburban Newspapers, and The Biology Place. He has won numerous awards and fellowships for excellence in teaching. He has a B.A. from Wesleyan University, and an M.A. from Columbia University. He currently teaches in Port Chester public school district.

Copyright © 1999 by Classroom Connect, Inc.
URL: http://www.classroom.com
Email: connect@classroom.com
(800) 638-1639

Due to the evolving nature of the Internet, addresses published in this book may change after publication. We do our utmost to check their validity before going to press and cannot be held responsible for any changes or inappropriate material that may appear after publication.

Printed in the United States of America

2 3 4 5 6 7 8 9 10 - 02 01 00 99

Composition and Layout: David Avery
Design: John Svatek, Sam Gorgone
Special Consultant: Barbara Huston

ISBN: 0-932577-66-0

TABLE OF CONTENTS

INTRODUCTION

Mathematics need not exist in a vacuum, isolated from other disciplines. We must reach across borders and back into history to learn its lessons. The greatest mathematicians have also been great statesmen, artists, and scientists. Contemplate for a moment the contributions of Archimedes, DaVinci, and Newton. Their math was built on a foundation of culture, and the beauty they saw in numbers was a reflection of the natural world.

Math students need not spend all their time in chairs aimed at the chalkboard. The Internet is a great vehicle to spur inquiry and debate among them. There is something special about the relationship between mathematics and computers. The very language we use to describe computers reflects their quantitative qualities: "kilobytes,""megahertz," "vector display." It's hard to believe when we stumble upon a Web site filled with Escher prints and fractals that the phone line carrying them to us somehow translates them into, and back out of, just so many ones and zeros.

In this book we offer a range of mathematics topics appropriate to the secondary level, including arithmetic, geometry, algebra, trigonometry, statistics, and calculus. Each lesson is taught in a multidisciplinary context, linking math to history, engineering, science, and a multitude of other fields of human enterprise.

We also offer a range of instructional styles and ideas. Your students will cut and paste paper, read to each other, build models, cover the bulletin board, and visit amusement parks. By visiting Web sites, your class will link their studies in mathematics to so many realms of society, including culture, history, economics, industry, science, technology, and art...the list of links is huge.

As you demand more computers and faster Internet access from your school, and appropriate training, you may wish to read from The National Council of Teachers of Mathematics position statement on using technology in the learning and teaching of mathematics:

> *Every classroom where mathematics is taught should have at least one computer for demonstrations, data acquisition, and other student use at all times. Every school mathematics program should provide additional computers and other types of technology for individual, small-group, and whole-class use. The involvement of teachers by school systems to develop a comprehensive plan for the ongoing acquisition, maintenance, and upgrading of computers and other emerging technology for use at all grade levels is imperative. As new technology develops, school systems must be ready to adapt to the changes and constantly upgrade the hardware, software, and curriculum to ensure that the mathematics program remains relevant and current.*

Make sure to let your students take the lead in their own learning; you'll be surprised at how much they teach you. When the modem disconnects and the browser quits, you'll take satisfaction in having used the computer to teach some of the math its designers used to build it.

Marc Alan Rosner

1 Geometry

THE GEOMETRY OF VISUAL PERSPECTIVE

 ## Overview

Students will learn how artists use geometry to create the illusion of three dimensional space in two dimensional media.

 ## Time Frame

Initial Lesson: one 45-minute period or equivalent
Extensions: 1-2 periods

Objectives

• Interpret illustrations from a geometrical standpoint
• Identify specific geometric shapes and relations
  (e.g., "trapezoid," "parallel")
• Link geometry to art, in an historical context

 ## Materials

• Pencil
• Ruler
• Paper
• Tracing paper
• Illustrated art books
• Protractor

# Procedure

1 Go to this site with students and read the tutorial on perspective, viewing the drawings in conjunction with the explanation:

WEB SITE 1. Perspective Drawing

•Ask students to respond to questions in Step A of Activity Sheet now.

2 Toward the bottom of the page, there is a problem asking you to draw a railroad track based on some images. Try this activity with your students, and then click to the "solution" page with them to check your work.

WEB SITE 2. Solutions to the RR Track Problem

3 Lead a discussion with students on the geometry of perspective. Look around the classroom and out the window to identify clear examples. Furniture, walls, and buildings have parallel lines and apparent vanishing points. The human brain perceives depth and perspective by monitoring the focus and angle of the eyes, and also by the shapes of objects and the orientation of lines and planes.

Discuss the evolution of art and development of perspective in artistic renderings. Little perspective is evident in ancient cave paintings and hieroglyphics; modern artists know about perspective and often employ it. Sculpture, perhaps by definition, occupies three dimensions; but artists working on paper and canvas require special strategies to trick the brain into perceiving depth.

•Students may now complete steps b & c of the Activity Sheet.

☼ Extensions

1 Visit this site and identify as many mathematical objects as you can in these pictures. Students should try to find line combinations that produce linear perspective:

WEB SITE **3. Albrecht Durer's engraving Melencolia I**

WEB SITE **4. Albrecht Durer's St. Jermome dans sa Cellule**

2 Students can use tracing paper to capture the important lines in art illustrations. "Deconstruct" the artist's use of perspective by measuring the length and angle of these lines. You can use the following image as an excellent example. The goal should be to find the vanishing point.

WEB SITE **5. The Vault of St. Ignazio**

3 Have students make perspective drawings of their own. They should begin by drawing the important lines and angles. Their use of line lengths and angles should be very deliberate and controlled, employing the geometric rules described in the lesson.

4 For an excellent explanation of linear perspective and dimension, go to the following. Use this site as a lesson starter. Let your students explore chiaroscuro, "the dramatic emphasis of light and shadow." Let students emphasize perspective by shading the shadow areas.

WEB SITE **6. The On-Line Visual Literacy Project**

THE GEOMETRY OF VISUAL PERSPECTIVE

NAME:_____

CLASS: _____ DATE:_____

Step   A   Go to this site and answer the questions on a separate piece of paper:

1. Perspective Drawing

1. What is the "vanishing point" in drawings?
2. What term describes figures which appear different in size but have the same shape and proportions as one another?
3. Historically, when and where was perspective introduced into art in a realistic way?
4. If you view a window from directly in front, what is its apparent geometric shape?
5. If you view a window from an angle, what is its apparent geometric shape?

Step   B   Consider and answer the hallway question. Check your solution at this site:

2. Solution to the Hallway Problem

6. In the first image in the hallway solution, name some line pairs which are supposedly parallel in real life.
7. What is the relationship between lines BD and XZ?
8. AB and AD are two segments which form the corner of a window. Their actual angle is 90°, called a right angle. Name another set of perpendicular segments.

Step   C   Study this famous engraving and write a paragraph analyzing the artist's geometric use of perspective. Describe which lines are parallel in real life, identify geometric figures apparent in the scene, and find the vanishing point.

4. Albrecht Durer's St. Jerome dans sa Cellule

TESSELLATIONS & ESCHER PATTERNS

Overview

In this activity, students will learn what a tessellation is. They'll identify the geometric figures at the basis of tessellations, learn about symmetry, and see how artists use tessellations in their work to create beauty and induce intrigue.

Time Frame

Initial Lesson: one 45-minute period or equivalent
Extensions: 2 periods

Objectives

- Identify and analyze tessellations
- Find axes of symmetry
- Recognize mathematical themes in art work

Materials

- Paper
- Ruler
- Scissors
- OPTIONAL: Plastic templates, available from educational supply catalogs; or bathroom and kitchen tiles

Procedure

❶ Define "tessellation" for students. Tessellation is the process of covering a plane by the repeated tiling of a regular polygon, such as a triangle, square, or hexagon. Tessellations are evident in the patterns of tiles found in kitchens, bathrooms, and on streets and buildings. See what tessellations you can identify in your school environment.

For a more sophisticated discussion of the definition of tessellation, go to this site and see what Suzanne Alejandre and Dr. Math have to say:

WEB SITE 1. What is a Tessellation?

❷ At the heart of tessellations is symmetry. Symmetry can take many forms. Some simple examples:
- The letter "A" has a vertical axis of symmetry.
- The letter "H" has both vertical and horizontal axes of symmetry.
- The letter "O" has multiple axes of symmetry.

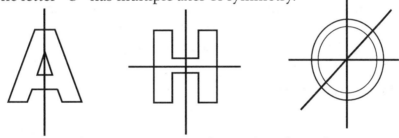

What kinds of symmetry can students identify in the polygons that tessellate the surfaces you studied in procedure step 1? For a more complex discussion on four types of symmetry in the plane, go to this site:

WEB SITE 2. The Four Types of Symmetry in the Plane

❸ Some artists use tessellations in their work, often to create optical illusions. The most famous artist to do this is undoubtedly the Dutch graphic artist M.C. Escher. His twentieth century works play with patterns, angles, and depth, often presenting the viewer with situations which are three-dimensionally impossible and frustrating to comprehend:

WEB SITE 3. Welcome to the M.C. Escher Annotated Gallery

WEB SITE 4. Our M.C. Escher Gallery

Other artists have followed suit:

WEB SITE 5. Escher Patterns by Yoshiaki Araki

Extensions

❶ Investigating tessellations using activity pattern blocks:

WEB SITE 6. Investigating Tessellations Using Activity Pattern Blocks

❷ Visit the World of Escher Store to see products emblazoned with the artist's famous works:

WEB SITE 7. World of Escher Gift Shop

❸ Do a large-scale tessellation layout on your bulletin board or on the gym floor using construction paper or poster-board.

❹ This page contains explanations of tessellations and transformations like those used in M. C. Escher's work. There are instructions for creating tessellations with Java. Also included is a lesson plan to use with your students.

WEB SITE 8. ArtMath Transformations

TESSELLATIONS & ESCHER PATTERNS

NAME:_____

CLASS: _____ DATE:_____

Step A Draw axes of symmetry through the following objects:

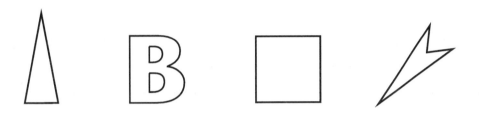

Step B Identify the fundamental polygons used in each of these tessellations. How many sides in each?

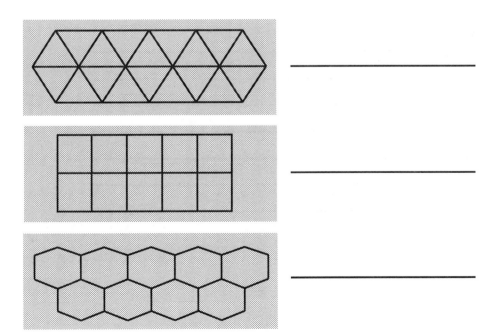

_____

_____

_____

WEB SITE **4. Our Escher Gallery**

Pick two works of Escher that depict scenes which could not really exist in three dimensions. Give a mathematical explanation of why they are impossible. Cite mathematical principles and postulates. For instance, the angles in a triangle add up to 180 degrees.

TITLE OF WORK:

_____

EXPLANATION:

_____

_____

_____

_____

_____

_____

TITLE OF WORK:

_____

EXPLANATION:

_____

_____

_____

_____

_____

_____

_____

Step **D** Go online and create your own tiling pattern that covers the plane. Roger Penrose, a noted British mathematical physicist and cosmologist, invented a special pattern feature that makes it different from other tessellations. Go to the Quasitiler to make some Penrose tilings of your own.

WEB SITE **9. Quasitiler**

WEB SITE **10. Penrose Tiling**

WEB SITE **11. The Geometry Junkyard**

What is special about Penrose's tiling system, and how does it compare to the tessellations you studied earlier?

_____

_____

_____

_____

_____

_____

_____

_____

_____

_____

THE PYTHAGOREAN THEOREM

Overview

The Pythagorean Theorem is probably the most famous theorem in all of mathematics. It has an elegant simplicity, yet arises in so many important applications. Students will prove the theorem a number of ways, generate Pythagorean triples, and solve problems using this famous formula.

Time Frame

Initial Lesson: two 45-minute periods or equivalent
Extensions: 4 periods

Objectives

•Construct proofs
•Apply algorithms

Materials

•Colored paper
•Scissors
•Glue
•SPECIAL BROWSER NEEDS: Frames; MPEG viewer such as Sparkle
•OPTIONAL: Java; Geometer Sketchpad 3.0

 # Procedure

1 Teach students the Pythagorean theorem and give them some sample Pythagorean triples.

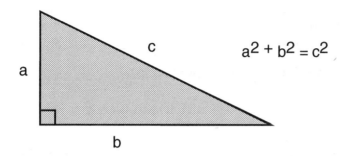

This theorem holds that the sum of the squares of the legs of a right triangle equals the square of the hypotenuse.

The simplest Pythagorean Triple—whole number integers that could be the sides of a right triangle—is 3, 4, 5. Plug into the formula to show that three squared plus four squared does indeed equal five squared. Multiplying this triple by whole numbers gives rise to others (e.g., 6, 8, 10); but there are others such as 5, 12, 13.

2 View the animation at this site to show students a visual proof of the Pythagorean Theorem. Ask students to explain why this shows the Pythagorean theorem to be true. They will be performing this proof using colored paper and scissors. For the students to be successful all they will need is the basic formula for area and some imagination.

WEB SITE **1. Animated Proof of the Pythagorean Theorem**

3 Work through one or more of the proofs, step-by-step, at this site. Make sure the students write down all of their statements and reasons of each proof:

WEB SITE **2. Interactive Mathematics Miscellany and Puzzles**

Select Item 5, Geometry, and then Items 41 or 42, Pythagoras'
Theorem. The first proof is an applet requiring Java ; subsequent
proofs can be read on-screen or printed.

Extensions

1 If you have a JavaScript capable browser, try this site. It
generates Pythagorean triples for you:

WEB SITE **3. Pythagorean Triple Calculator in JavaScript**

2 If you have Geometer's Sketchpad, try this nice lesson plan by
Janet Mae Zahumeny:

WEB SITE **4. Lesson Plan**

3 Take your students back in time by having them explore an
ancient proof of the Pythagorean theorem. This proof is proposition 47 of book 1 of Euclid's Elements. If you have a Java-capable
browser, your students will actually be able to manipulate the
diagram of this proof, testing for its validity.

WEB SITE **5. Euclid's Elements, Book 1 Proposition 47**

4 Let your students explore the history of the age that produced
math's most famous theorem. Pythagoras and his society will
captivate your class with their forward thinking philosophies in
such an ancient time.

WEB SITE **6. Pythagoras of Samos**

THE PYTHAGOREAN THEOREM

NAME: _____

CLASS: _____ DATE:_____

Step A Find the length of the unknown side in the triangles pictured. You may have to express some answers in terms of a square root. In each case, show all work as you solve the problem.

1)

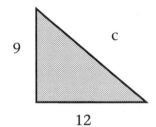

9
c
12

2)

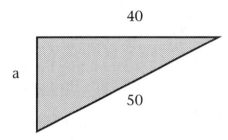

40
a
50

3)

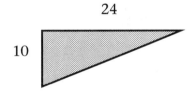

24
10

4)

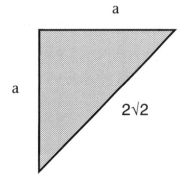

a
a
2√2

(isoceles; a=b)

Step B Go to this site and read the description of how Pythagorean triples can be generated:

3. Pythagorean Triple Calculator in JavaScript

Given two integers, s and t, you can generate Pythagorean triples x, y, & z as follows:

$$x = 2st$$

$$y = t^2 - s^2$$

$$z = t^2 + s^2$$

For example, if s=5 and t=6, you get a Pythagorean triple of 60, 9, and 61. Assign integer values to s and t to generate three new Pythagorean triples not encountered previously in this lesson; then use the Pythagorean theorem to prove they are indeed Pythagorean triples.

Challenge your students to find as many Pythagorean triples as they can using the procedure above. They should be aware that they will be responsible for showing all work in computing these large numbers. So they should choose integers s and t very carefully. They must show their calculations for finding the Pythagorean triples and also for proving their validity using the Pythagorean Theorem.

Step C Go to this site and print out the images on the page: Your students will be using the shapes on this page to manually perform a proof of the Pythagorean Theorem.

1. Animated Proof of the Pythagorean Theorem

Cut along the perimeters of the pictured polygons with scissors with a partner, and rearrange them in the manner depicted by the animation.

Draw a right triangle on the chalkboard. Then tell your students to draw their own right triangles on a piece of paper. Students create three squares similar to the diagram below using colored paper. Now using the same method as in Step C, tell them to fit the two smaller squares over the larger square.

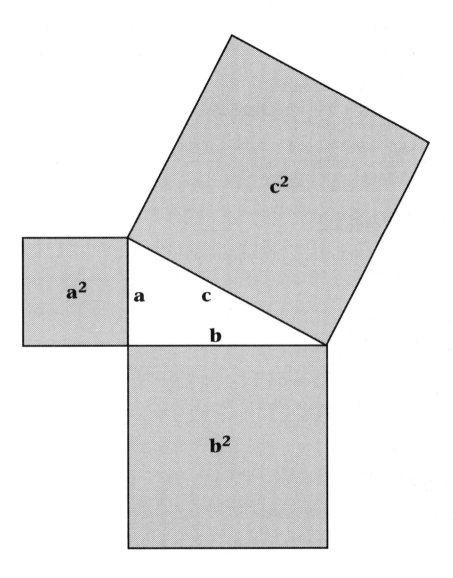

POLYGONS AND POLYHEDRA

Overview

In this exercise, students will learn about planar polygons and three-dimensional polyhedra. They'll solve problems based on these geometrical constructs, and visualize them using the advanced graphics capabilities of computers.

Time Frame

Initial Lesson: one 45-minute period or equivalent
Extensions: 2 periods

Objectives

• Define polygon and polyhedron
• Learn formula linking number of sides of a regular polygon to measure of interior angles
• Extend geometry of 2-D polyhedra to 3-D space

Materials

• Protractor
• Ruler
• Compass
• Paper
• Tape

Procedure

1 Polygons are two-dimensional constructs. They exist on a plane. "Poly" means "many;" "Polygon" means "many-sided" figure. Let students generate a list of polygons, including:

- Name of polygon.
- Number of sides.
- Representative sketch.
- Examples of use of each in architecture, art, or design.

Focus on regular polygons, in order of increasing number of sides, including: equilateral triangle; square; pentagon; hexagon; heptagon; octagon; nonagon; decagon.
You can enhance your discussion with the tutorials at these sites, which take the topic into great depth:

WEB SITE **1. Polygons**

WEB SITE **2. Geometry Center Lesson 5: Polygons**

WEB SITE **3. Geometry Center Lesson 5.3: Regular Polygons**

2 Polyhedrons are three-dimensional objects surfaced by polygons. Help students generate a list of polyhedra, as you did with polygons in step 1. You'll find students are less familiar with polyhedra structure and names. Simple polyhedra include the four-sided tetragon; five-sided pyramid; six-sided cube. Some students have difficulty visualizing three-dimensional constructs, so it helps to have models on hand, or to make them.

Take a colorful ride into the world of polyhedra by viewing the beautiful images at this site:

WEB SITE **4. Virtual Polyhedra**

3 Note that although your discussion has been on regular polygons and polyhedra, there are irregular ones as well. A trapezoid is an example of a polygon which is not regular (equal-sided). Note also that length can be used to represent the sides of polygons and edges of polyhedra; area can be used to represent the surface of polygons and polyhedra; and volume is the measure of the space a polyhedron occupies.

Extensions

1 Send your students on a real scavenger hunt looking for ten geometrical constructs on the school grounds. They can write the location of each of the following shapes that are found.
Items to be found:
a right triangle, a square, a cube, an equilateral triangle, a hexagon, a 45° angle, an octagon, a tetrahedron (pyramid), a rectangle that is not a square, and a pentagon or heptagon.

WEB SITE **1. Polygons**

WEB SITE **4. Virtual Polyhedra**

2 Get hands-on and construct polyhedra with classroom materials. Tell your students that you are making dice for a game. The dice can be 16-sided, 20-sided, or whatever they can think to make:

WEB SITE **5. Paper Polyhedra**

3 If you have VRML (Virtual Reality Modeling Language) software on your machine, study this set of polyhedra:

WEB SITE **6. The Five Platonic Solids**

4 Hungry for more? You'll find dozens of polyhedron links here:

WEB SITE **7. George W. Hart's Pavilion of Polyhedreality**

POLYGONS AND POLYHEDRA

NAME: _____

CLASS: _____ DATE:_____

Step A Complete the following table describing regular polygons. Base your answers on information you find at these sites:

WEB SITE 1. Polygons

WEB SITE 3. Lesson 5.3: Regular Polygons

NAME	SIDES	INTERIOR ANGLE	EXAMPLES
triangle	3	60°	side of tent
	4		side of box
pentagon		108°	
		120°	bathroom tiles
octagon	8		

Step B On a separate paper find the area of the depicted polygons, given the following formulas. Show your work:

area of a triangle = ½bh
area of a square = s²
area of a trapezoid = ½(b₁+b₂)h

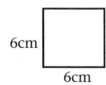
6cm

6cm

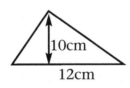
10cm

12cm

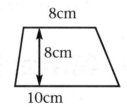
12cm

6cm

8cm

8cm

10cm

Step C In a paragraph or two, describe polygons and polyhedra visible at this site:

WEB SITE 8. Quick Tour of MathMol

MATHEMATICS & MOLECULES

 ## Overview

Chemistry is a fabulous springboard for studying mathematics. Scientists describe atoms and molecules comprehensively with quantitative data. The atomic number and mass of atoms, and the specific angle, at which they bond, determine the nature of matter and life in the universe.

 ## Time Frame

Initial Lesson: one 45-minute period or equivalent
Extensions: 1-2 periods

Objectives

•Calculate angles
•Identify geometric relationships between atoms in molecules
•Relate mathematics to chemistry

 ## Materials

•OPTIONAL: Organic molecule modeling kit; protractor

 **Procedure**

1 Give a quick "chemistry" lesson, focusing on the mathematics of some simple inorganic substances. Water—H_2O—is a three-atom molecule. It contains one oxygen and two hydrogens, at approximately a 105° angle.

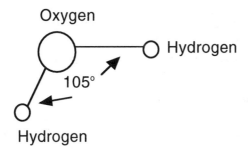

In their most common isotopes, hydrogen has one proton and one electron, and oxygen has eight protons and eight electrons. The atomic number of an atom equals the number of protons. The atomic number plus the number of neutrons equals the mass number. The number of electrons equals the number of protons in a neutral atom.

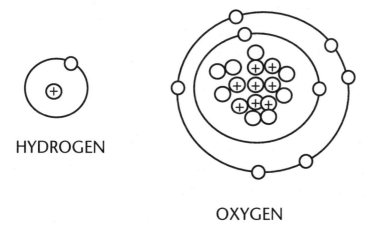

HYDROGEN

OXYGEN

To summarize for a neutral atom:

> ATOMIC NUMBER determines element type, equals number of protons.
> MASS NUMBER equals protons plus electrons.
> A Number of ELECTRONS equals number of protons.

Bonding results from sharing and exchanging electrons. Visit this site for quantitative data on each element:

🌐 **1. Periodic Table of the Elements**

2 We can identify the angles in other molecules. Show students some of the images at this site, paying specific attention to the number of atoms and bonds, and the bond angles:

🌐 **2. Quick Tour of MathMol**

Benzene rings are hexagonal rings of 6 carbon atoms. In a planar hexagonal arrangement, the bond angle is 120°. Ammonia (NH_3) is another molecule with 120° angles. Adding a fourth substrate (group) to an atom often results in a tetragonal arrangement; CCl_4 has bond angles of 109°.

NH_3
triagonal planar
120° bonds

CCl_4
tetragonal
109° bonds

🎲 Extensions

1 Another virtual periodic table with lots of data is located at this site: This site gives information about each element by just clicking on the element in the table. Also register for a copy of this site on CD for your own computer.

🌐 **3. WebElements**

2 Use organic chemistry model kits and protractors to analyze the angles in different carbon molecules. Chemistry Visualized uses these beautiful movies and images to discuss the basics of Physical and General Chemistry. Instruct your students to examine how molecules bond and form patterns similar to polyhedrons.

🌐 **4. Chemistry Visualized**

Activity Sheet 5

MATHEMATICS & MOLECULES

NAME: _____

CLASS: _____ DATE:_____

Step A Go to this site:

WEB SITE **5. The Hydrocarbons Page**

Complete this table for the number of atoms in various carbon alkane (carbon-hydrogen) chains:

NAME	NUMBER OF CARBONS	NUMBER OF ATOMS
methane	1	5
	2	8
propane		11
	4	14
pentane		17
hexane	6	
heptane	7	
octane		26

Step B Now figure out a mathematical formula, f(n), which gives the total number of atoms in an alkane as a function of n, the number of carbon atoms.

Step C Browse the water section and molecules of life section of MathMol, and write a composition describing the geometry of the different atoms and compounds you encounter. What characteristic angles arise repeatedly? Pay attention to consistent types of bonds (e.g., C-H-C). How can you tell bond angle measures from two-dimensional images and 3-D animations? Note the general color scheme: carbon atoms are green; hydrogen, white; oxygen, blue; etc.

WEB SITE **6. Water Section**

WEB SITE **7. Molecules of Life Page**

Number Concepts

Pi π

Overview

Pi is certainly the most famous irrational number. It is defined most frequently as the ratio of a circle's circumference to its diameter, but arises in dozens of other ways in the field of mathematics. In this activity, students will learn about the application of Pi to mathematical problems, and the historical refinement of the known value of this constant.

Time Frame

Initial Lesson: two 45-minute periods or equivalent
Extensions: 2 periods

Objectives

• Use Pi to solve problems
• Trace historical discovery and refinement of Pi
• Appreciate significance of Pi from different perspectives

Materials

• Measuring tape
• String
• Cans and cylindrical box tops
• Scrap or construction paper

 # Procedure

1 Read this short home page:

WEB SITE 1. Pi Mathematics

Note the links to different areas in this Pi-rich site.

2 Pi has a value of approximately 3.14. The three best known formulas using Pi are:

$$C = \pi D \qquad\qquad C = 2\pi r \qquad\qquad A = \pi r^2$$

Where π = Pi
C = the circumference of a circle
D = the diameter of a circle
A = the area of a circle

Teach these formulas to your students and then try the excellent tutorial and problems with them at this page:

WEB SITE 2. Pi Application

Students can solve problems in turn at the board or in small groups and can check their answers at the site.

Pi is one of an infinite class of irrational numbers. An irrational number is one which can not be expressed simply as a ratio of whole numbers. It's an infinitely long decimal that never repeats and has no apparent pattern. Other examples of irrational numbers include the square root of 2, and "e."

3 Do the hands-on activities at this site:

WEB SITE 3. Activities for Pi Mathematics

Students will make physical measurements in order to calculate Pi themselves.

☼ Extensions

1 Surprisingly, there are several formulae that use the Fibonacci numbers to compute Pi! Here's a brief introduction to all you need to know to appreciate these:

WEB SITE 4. Pi and the Fibonacci Numbers

2 Learn about Archimedes' calculation of Pi here:

WEB SITE 5. Graphics for the Calculus Classroom

3 Using scrap or construction paper, cut out the digits of Pi and put them up in the hallway outside your classroom. You can take Pi all the way to the principal's office; this page provides it to a thousand places:

WEB SITE 6. Pi to 1000 Places

4 Look and listen to Pi in different ways at this clever site:

WEB SITE 7. Elias' Pi Page

Pi π

NAME: _____

CLASS: _____ DATE:_____

Step **A** Read through this site and answer the
questions below:

WEB SITE **8. History of Pi**

1. Complete this table showing the number of known decimal places
   for Pi through the ages:

   DATE   # OF DECIMAL PLACES
   500 BC
   800 AD   <u>4 places</u>
   1600 AD   _____
   1990 AD   _____
            _____

2. Give three historic values of Pi which were close but inaccurate; note
   who determined the value, when, and how.

Historic Value of Pi	Measurer	Time Period	Method

3. Approximate Pi as two different ratios of whole numbers:

   _____/_____   _____/_____

Step B Complete the following table of circle data using Pi formulas you know, and using 3.14 for π.

CIRCLE RADIUS	DIAMETER	CIRCUMFERENCE	AREA
1 cm	2 cm	6.28 cm	3.14 cm
3		18.84	
	10		78.5
	20		

Step C Now complete the following problems twice. For the first set of problems use a proposed value of π to be 3. Then complete the problems again using the value of π to be 3.141529.

1. $\pi =3$ (Show your work!)

a. Find the area of a circle with diameter 12.

b. Find the circumference of a circle with diameter 12.

c. What happens to the area of this circle if we double the diameter.

d. What happens to the circumference if we double the diameter.

2. $\pi =3.14159$ (Show your work!)

a. Find the area of a circle with diameter 12.

b. Find the circumference of a circle with diameter 12.

c. What happens to the area of this circle if we double the diameter.

d. What happens to the circumference if we double the diameter.

3. Notice what changes when using different values of π. Do the math operations and concepts change? What stays the same? What is different?

_____

_____

_____

_____

_____

In the USA the value of Pi gave rise to heated political debate. In the State of Indiana in 1897 the House of Representatives unanimously passed a Bill introducing a new mathematical truth:

Be it enacted by the General Assembly of the State of Indiana: It has been found that a circular area is to the square on a line equal to the quadrant of the circumference, as the area of an equilateral rectangle is to the square of one side. (Section I, House Bill No. 246, 1897).

In other words, why get complicated over the value of Pi? Why not just round it to 3? Imagine for a moment that the U.S. Government passed a law mandating that 3, exactly, be used for Pi. Write a paragraph describing how that would affect society, culture, technology, and industry.

_____

_____

_____

_____

_____

_____

_____

_____

_____

_____

_____

_____

_____

_____

FIBONACCI SEQUENCES

Overview

Fibonacci sequences are strings of numbers famous both in mathematics and science. Students will study the functions that generate such sequences and their relevance to the natural world.

Time Frame

Initial Lesson: one 45-minute period or equivalent
Extensions: 2-3 periods

Objectives

•Identify functions of real numbers
•Distinguish between algebraic and geometric progressions
•Study the manifestation of mathematics in nature

Materials

•Pencil and ruler
•Standard calculator

# Procedure

❶ Discuss the classic Fibonacci sequence below. However, don't give students all the terms; give them the first four or five and have them generate the rest together as a class:

0, 1, 1, 2, 3, 5, 8, 13, 21, 34, 55...
Determine with them the function which provides this sequence:

$$f(n) = f(n-1) + f(n-2)$$

❷ Go to this site:

WEB SITE **1. Fibonacci Numbers and Nature**

Read about Fibonacci's Rabbits, a hypothetical thought-experiment which illustrates the relevance of this sequence of numbers to nature. Note the underlying assumptions at the core of this example; e.g., the premise that the rabbits reach reproductive maturity at two months of age; that all rabbits reproduce when old enough; that they keep living indefinitely with no natural restrictions.

❸ Continue the discussion with students in greater depth. How do Fibonacci sequences differ from other progressions?

Algebraic or arithmetic: 3, 6, 9, 12, 15, 18...
Geometric: 1, 2, 4, 8, 16, 32...

An algebraic or arithmetic series proceeds by the addition of a constant value (3 in the example above). A geometric series proceeds by the multiplication of a constant ratio (2 in the example above).

What other algebraic and geometric series can students construct? Notice that the series above are based upon integers. Where an integer equals n, the function of the above series are, respectively:

$$f(n) = 3n$$
$$f(n) = 2^n$$

As students will read on their own, the limit of the ratio of two neighboring numbers in a Fibonacci sequence as n approaches infinity is known as the "golden ratio," with implications for architecture, art, and other disciplines.

⚙ Extensions

❶ Dr. Knott has much more to offer than bunnies at his main site on Fibonacci Numbers:

🌐 **2. Fibonacci Numbers and the Golden Section**

Here you can study the general mathematics of Fibonacci numbers, Fibonacci puzzles, and the Golden Mean.

❷ Students can post the Fibonacci sequence in large numbers along the hallway outside your class. Passersby can try to guess what they mean. (The Guggenheim museum in New York City did this on the side of their building in neon lights several years ago. Drivers and pedestrians on Fifth Avenue were left to wonder.)

❸ Challenge your students to use the Golden Ratio in a drawing of their own. Have your students go to the following site to see examples of this ratio used in art and architecture. Then set them to the task of basing a sketch or original artwork on the Golden Ratio.

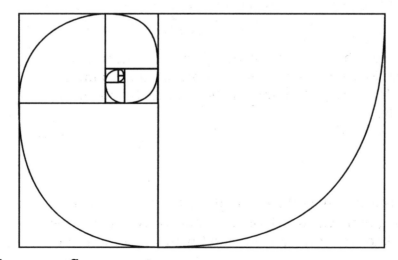

FIBONACCI SEQUENCES

NAME: _____

CLASS: _____ DATE:_____

(WEB SITE) 3. The Golden Section in Art, Architecture and Music

Step A Give the next two numbers in the following series, and express the associated functions in the form "f(n)=..."

1.)   4, 8, 12, 16, 20, 24, ___, ___...   f(n)= _____
2.)   3, 9, 27, 81, ___, ___...   f(n)= _____
3.)   1, 4, 9, 16, 25, 36, ___, ___...   f(n)= _____

Step B Go to this site and answer the questions below:

(WEB SITE) 1. Fibonacci Numbers and Nature

4.) What is the "golden ratio" ("golden mean")?

_____

_____

5.) Look at the series of squares used to generate the Fibonacci Spiral. Consider the total area as each square is added. Complete the next three numbers in this series of the total area:

1, 2, 6, 15, ___, ___, ___

Step C Finish reading this site, and give three examples of how Fibonacci's sequence manifests itself in nature. On a separate sheet of paper name the example, and explain how his sequence arises.

Logic & Games

 ## Overview

Math games are fun but also the basis of serious research. Mathematicians analyze games to help engineer computer configurations, military strategies, financial projections, encryption processes, and a host of other applications.

 ## Time Frame

Initial Lesson: one 45-minute period or equivalent
Extensions: 2-4 periods

Objectives

•Learn logic terms
•Categorize basic logical statements
•Have fun doing math

 ## Materials

•No special materials needed

 # Procedure

1 Introduce students to some basic logic terms (such as statement and argument). Mission Critical cites examples with explanations to help students with the basics. Be sure to include some of the exercises on this site to warm them up.

WEB SITE 1. Mission Critical

Discuss the "if p, then q" style representation of statements. For example:

p: "it is raining"
q: "you go out with your umbrella"
p → q (if p, then q): If it is raining, you go out with your umbrella.

If that statement is taken to be true, a logical consequence of this is ~q → ~p (if not q, then not p): If you do not go out with your umbrella, then it is not raining.

At the Introduction to Logic Web page you can lead your students through an introduction to the "if-then" structure. Read the material and perform some of the corresponding exercises with your class.

WEB SITE 2. Introductions to Conditional Arguments

2 While your students are surfing through these sites instruct
them to write down terms and definitions that are new to them.
Analyze the specific examples given at the above sites. Make
note of the following terms:

- Antecedent
- Consequent
- Syllogism
- Dilemma
- Contrary
- Contradictory

Have students construct some logic statements of their own,
analogous to the given examples. The students should be able to
classify the parts of their statements by concepts that they have
seen in this lesson.

Extensions

1 Here is an exercise in problem solving involving combinations
in a clever interactive game. Do not let them go to the answer
Web page until they have formulated conclusions on how to
win this game:

WEB SITE 3. The Fruit Game Home Page

2 If you have a Java-capable browser, you'll enjoy the cutting-edge
interactive fun at this site:

WEB SITE 4. Marcia's Games

3 Visit this site for a lesson in rule-based reason:

WEB SITE 5. Two Logic Puzzles

4 Haven't had enough? The Math Forum offers this site of puzzle
and problem links:

WEB SITE 6. Math Problems & Puzzles

LOGIC & GAMES

NAME: _____

CLASS: _____ DATE:_____

Step   A Go to this site:

WEB SITE **2. Introduction to Conditional Arguments**

Determine whether each argument is valid or invalid. Circle your
choice for each argument.

1. If it is raining, I will take my umbrella.
   It is raining, so I'll take my umbrella.

       Valid   Invalid

2. If Jennifer is late, she will miss the movie.
   Jennifer missed the movie, so she must have been late.

       Valid   Invalid

3. If a visitor to the museum is under 10 years old, he or she will get a discount.
   Miguel is 8 years old, so he will get a discount.

       Valid   Invalid

4. If a visitor to the museum is under 10 years old, he or she will get a discount.
   Rhonda got a discount. She must be under 10 years old.

       Valid   Invalid

5. If the bike is red, then it belongs to me.
   That bike is blue, so it does not belong to me.

       Valid   Invalid

6. If an animal is an amphibian, then it can live in water.
   A frog is an amphibian. A frog can live in water.

       Valid   Invalid

7. Introduction to Conditional Chain Arguments

Classify each of the statements below as one of the following:

- Modus Ponens (Affirming the Antecedent)
- Modus Tollens (Denying the Consequent)
- Affirming the Consequent
- Denying the Antecedent

7. When it's cold, you wear a jacket. So if you're not wearing a jacket, it must not be cold.

_____

8. If summer comes, it will get warmer. Since summer is coming, it will get warm.

_____

9. If I'm driving I'm in a car. I'm not driving, so I'm not in a car.

_____

10. All dogs are animals; so all animals must be dogs.

_____

Step **C** Devise examples of each of the following. Construct your own statements or sets of statements. Then indicate whether each statement is necessarily true or false.

- Modus Ponens (Affirming the Antecedent)

_____

- Modus Tollens (Denying the Consequent)

_____

- Affirming the Consequent

_____

- Denying the Antecedent

_____

Step D Using the Web site above conclude answers for the questions from the exercises in Conditional Chain Arguments. Explain your answers completely in writing.

7. Exercises for Conditional Chain Arguments

1. What can you conclude if the Senator wins the New Hampshire primary? Why?

_____

_____

_____

_____

2. What can you conclude if the Senator is not elected president? Why?

_____

_____

_____

_____

3. What can you conclude if the Senator does not win the nomination? Why?

_____

_____

_____

_____

_____

4. If the Senator does not have an advantage in campaign fund-raising, can he be elected president? Why?

_____

_____

_____

_____

_____

PRIME NUMBERS

Overview

A prime number is a number divisible only by itself and one. Although the concept of prime numbers is fairly simple, books have been written about this huge field of mathematics. Prime numbers have applications in many fields, from number theory to cryptography.

Time Frame

Initial Lesson: one 45-minute period or equivalent
Extensions: 3 periods

Objectives

•Learn definition of prime number
•Generate primes
•Learn history and importance of prime numbers

Materials

•No special materials needed

# Procedure

1 Introduce prime numbers by giving the definition and by listing the first few. Primes are those numbers which can not be factored into anything aside from themselves and unity (1). Give students the first few prime numbers and have them generate some more:

2, 3, 5, 7, 11, 13, 17, 19, 23, 29, 31, 37, 41, 43...

When they tire of this, let them take a peek at the first ten thousand prime numbers:

WEB SITE 1. The First 10,000 Primes

Non-prime numbers have more than two factors:

6 has factors 1, 2, 3, 6.
100 has factors 1, 2, 4, 5, 10, 20, 25, 50, and 100.

2 The Greeks proved that there is no upper limit to prime numbers; the set is infinite. Of course, not all prime numbers known were discovered by trial-and-error factoring. There are methods and formulas for generating primes. See if students can devise any systematic way of finding primes. A site is devoted to this topic:

WEB SITE 2. Finding Primes and Proving Primality

3 Of what use are prime numbers? Well, the government, for one, has a vested interest in them. It seems that primes are useful for cryptography: scrambling and unscrambling messages. Say that you want to order something over the computer using your credit card. Is there a way of sending your card number in code so that someone can't intercept and use it? Yes...the computer can use software to mix it up, and the receiving computer has a mathematical "key" to unscramble it. It turns out that prime numbers—large ones—are useful for making the keys for encryption. The task of factoring these huge numbers is part of breaking the codes of encrypted messages. A famous encryption method called "RSA," using a very large prime number, was "cracked" [decoded] recently by thousands of computers working in parallel over the Internet, in a contest.

☼ Extensions

1 You'll find tons of information on prime numbers and related links at this site. Explore your students' writing abilities with a writing assignment researched at this site. The title of the piece can be "Prime numbers are important because...." Some topics might include: the role of prime numbers in the set of integers, the historical significance of prime numbers, or even the reason brilliant men toiled millions of hours studying their importance.

WEB SITE 3. The Prime Page

2 Join over 1300 of your fellow number-theory enthusiasts in the search for new Mersenne primes! As in the RSA-130 factoring project, the power of hundreds of small computers like yours can be used to solve seemingly intractable problems.

WEB SITE 4. The GREAT Internet Mersenne Prime Search

3 A fun activity to challenge your student is to have them create the Sieve of Eratosthenes. Your students can go to this site for the step-by-step instructions that will show how this famous mathematician devised this prime number algorithm. Of course your students should be asked to describe how this method works orally or in writing.

WEB SITE 5. Finding Primes: Sieve of Eratosthenes

4 Add an exciting element to your prime number lesson with a free software program to find primes on your computer. You can download this freeware at the following site. Have your students experiment with finding large primes using the software.

WEB SITE 6. Mersenne Prime Freeware

PRIME NUMBERS

NAME: _____

CLASS: _____ DATE: _____

Step   A   On a separate sheet of paper, factor the following numbers using a "factor tree." The first one has been done for you. (You need not list 1 or the number itself.)

24: _____

35: _____

50: _____

 8: _____

$$18$$
$$2 \quad\quad 9$$
$$3 \quad\quad 3$$

Factors are 2,3,3,9

Step   B   Go to this page and read through it; then answer the questions below:

WEB SITE 7. Prime Numbers

1. What is a perfect number? Give an example.

_____

2. How many prime numbers exist?

_____

3. What is the Fundamental Theorem of Algebra?

_____

4. Who showed that every prime number of the form $4^n + 1$ can be written in a unique way as the sum of two squares?

_____

5. True or false: All numbers of the form $2^n - 1$ are prime.

_____

6. List two problems (questions) about prime numbers which remain unanswered:

_____

Step   C   Use the function $f(n) = 2^n - 1$ to find five prime numbers between 0 and 500. Check that numbers are prime.

VIRTUAL DICE

 ## Overview

Students will study probability and statistics using "virtual dice," examining the distribution of sums that arise in the random toss of dice. They will extend their reasoning to other random acts such as tossing coins and drawing cards from a deck.

 ## Time Frame

Initial Lesson: two 45-minute periods or equivalent
Extensions: 2 periods

 ## Objectives

•Calculate probability of single events
•Calculate probability of combinations

 ## Materials

•Coins
•Dice
•Playing cards

# Procedure

1 Discuss probability of coin tosses and dice rolls with students. The odds a coin will come up heads is expressed in various ways:

- •fractional probability --------->one in two
- •decimal probability --------->0.5
- •percentage probability --------->50-50
- •probability as odds --------->one to one

2 Extend the conversation to the probability of a one-dice roll. The probability of a distinct number coming up in a die roll can be expressed in a variety of ways:

- • (as odds) five to one
- • (as a decimal) 0.167
- • (as a fraction) one in six

3 Now consider the roll of two dice. The probability of each individual die is the same. Have students figure out the greatest sum that could arise (12) and the least (2). Ask them if they know the likeliest (7). Then bring them to this site and run some trials of the "virtual dice" to confirm the probabilities discussed in this step and the previous one:

WEB SITE **1. Bill's World Virtual Dice**

First, focus on one die, the one on the left; then consider them in tandem.

Extensions

1 Students can use actual coins and dice to explore probability and statistics. Let them show that coins have a 0.5 probability of coming up on a particular side; the more trials they conduct, the clearer this becomes. Let them see how many heads in a row they can toss; the probability is raised to an additional exponent of two with each number. The odds of five heads in a row is one in two to the fifth power, or one in thirty-two. Dare them to flip a dozen heads in a row; it's not likely to happen even if a large class of students flips coins for an hour!

2 Students can try more sophisticated dice rolls at this site, varying the number of dice, the number of sides, etc.: Your students can use this random dice engine for a variety of data analysis exercises. Irony Game's Dice Server allows the user to customize exactly how many dice they need to roll, the number of sides on the dice, the number of rolls needed to be made, and they can even exclude the highest or lowest dice roll from the group. There are a variety of games that can be simulated in this manner.

🌐 2. Irony Game's Dice Server

3 Extend the discussion to playing cards. A normal deck has fifty-two cards—four suits of thirteen numbers each. What determines the rank of hands in poker? (pair, two pair, three of a kind, straight, flush, four of a kind, straight flush, royal flush)? The following site from Drexel University goes into the basics of game theory. Your students will be fascinated by the extensive role mathematics has in many games that they play.

🌐 3. Game Theory

4 A fun way to raise interest in probability is to apply the concepts to factors in their lives. Discuss some life events and their probabilities. Students love seeing what chances were involved for them to become like they are. Other topics like weather phenomenon or accidents may have them interested once they understand what the chances mean mathematically. Use this list for ideas:

- Gender of children.
- Sharing of birthdays.
- Inclement weather.
- Risks (tobacco, automobiles, lightning, sharks).
- State lottery games.

VIRTUAL DICE

NAME: _____

CLASS: _____ DATE:_____

Step A Imagine tossing two dice, and all the possible outcomes. Fill out the following table with the sums of each toss. Some have been done for you:

DIE A	1	2	3	4	5	6
DIE B						
1	2	4	__	__	__	__
2	3	__	__	__	__	__
3	__	__	__	__	__	__
4	__	__	__	__	__	__
5	__	__	8	__	__	__
6	__	__	__	__	__	12

Step B Now find the distribution of each total. That is, how many times does each possible number appear in your table in STEP A? Some have been done for you.

SUM	NUMBER OF APPEARANCES
2	1
3	2
4	__
5	__
6	__
7	__
8	5
9	__
10	__
11	__
12	__

WEB SITE **4. Irony Game's Dice Server**

•Set the number of dice to 2.
•Set the number of sides to 6.
•Do not add or subtract anything to the roll.
•Do not drop the highest or the lowest roll.
•Set the roll repeat to 20 times.

Now, roll the dice several times according to the parameters you just set. Record the numbers generated by the computer. Answer these questions based upon your findings:

1. What is the most common number you roll with dice? Explain why.

_____

_____

_____

_____

_____

_____

2. What are the least common numbers? Explain why.

_____

_____

_____

_____

_____

_____

3. What are the odds of tossing a coin "heads" three times in a row?

_____

_____

_____

_____

_____

_____

4. What are the odds of drawing a random card from a deck and having it be a diamond?

_____

_____

_____

_____

_____

_____

5. What are the odds of drawing a random card from a deck and having it be an ace?

_____

_____

_____

_____

_____

_____

6. What are the odds of drawing the four of hearts?

_____

_____

_____

_____

_____

_____

3 Real Life Math

CUSTOMER CENTS

Overview

It's not always easy to know how to be a smart consumer. In this activity students examine ads and sale policies to find out what's true, what's legal, what's not, and what rights a consumer has in various situations.

Time Frame

Initial Lesson: one 45-minute period or equivalent
Extensions: 2-3 periods

Objectives

- Identify an ad or advertising claim (print or broadcast) that seems confusing, raises a question, or seems too good to be true
- Mathematically evaluate the ad, or claim, to find out exactly what the store or manufacturer is offering and whether or not the store or manufacturer is acting honestly and legally
- Present the analysis as a report to the class

Materials

- Computer with Internet Access
- Newspaper or Magazines

# Procedure

1 Show students an ad or product claim from a local newspaper, or play an ad you taped from the radio or TV, or discuss a store's policy that seems shady or unfair. Ask them to analyze each ad or product claim by asking questions such as: What statement or claim is being made? (for example, "lowest prices in town") Have your students browse through the following Web page. This is a pamphlet for consumers put on the Web as a text file. Have your students perform the suggested exercises.

WEB SITE 1. Getting What You Pay For, Weights and Measures Tips For Consumers

2 Open this Web site where students can find examples of advertising scams that have been identified by their peers.

WEB SITE 2. Street Cents Online

First have students look at The Beef, about an ad some found questionable, and The Pit, about a shoddily made product.

3 Allow students a few days after their Internet trip to look at local newspapers, listen to radio and TV ads, or visit stores to find ads or product claims they want to investigate. Explain that they should investigate the truthfulness of ads and claims or the fairness of store policies through research or interviews.

WEB SITE 3. Consumer World

4 As a class solve the following type of puzzle that frequently challenges the math skills of consumers.
For example, assume the normal markup (increase in price over the merchant's cost) is 80% on an item whose list price is $78.50. The merchant is offering the item at $52.00 and claims that this is 10% over his cost. Is the merchant telling the truth?

Remind students to show all calculations and explain their conclusions. Let x equal the cost of the item to the merchant. Then:

$1.80x = \$78.50$

$x = \$78.50/1.80 = \$43.61$

10% of $43.61 = $4.36

So cost + 10% = $43.61 + $4.36 = $47.97

(The merchant is not telling the truth.)

⑤ Students should use the above model as the basis for their own reports which should include the following elements:
an explanation of the ad, claim, or policy that the student has questioned and researched and why the student questioned it; what a representative of the newspaper, broadcaster, ad agency, product maker, or store said when confronted with the problem; the results of student research and analysis that explains whether or not there is a legal or ethical problem with the ad, claim, or policy; what a consumer can or should do if he or she encounters the problem researched.

⊠ Extensions

① Invite students who are especially interested in the investigation of consumer scams to find out how the professionals do it. Let those students check out the online consumer magazines. Have students look for the magazines by name at Consumer World dealing with topics such as Consumer Information, Consumer Magazines, Consumer Affairs.

WEB SITE 3. Consumer World

② Check to see if your state or local office of consumer affairs has a Web site where the public can get information on consumer rights or learn how to register a complaint about a product or local business.

WEB SITE 4. Consumer Agencies

③ Encourage students, if such a site is available, to send information they've gathered about illegal or misleading ads and store policies to the site by e-mail or surface mail.
Be sure to post any reply so students can see how they can make a difference.

CUSTOMER CENTS

NAME: _____

CLASS: _____ DATE:_____

Step A Go to the Web sites below where you can find tips on becoming a smart consumer and a few examples of advertising scams identified by kids. Be prepared to answer questions from the "Tips" Web site that your teacher will give you.

 1. Getting What You Pay For, Weights and Measures Tips For Consumers

 2. Street Cents Online

On the home page of Street Cents Online, click on Forums at the bottom. Under What's Online on the next page, click on Bargain-mania. Next, look at Beef, about an ad some kids found questionable and Fit for the Pit, about a shoddily made product.

After visiting the Internet, take a few days to look at newspapers and listen to radio and TV ads, or look through stores to find ads or product claims you want to investigate.

Do your investigation about the truthfulness of ads and claims or the fairness of store policies with the help of some of these:

• interviews with people at local newspapers and radio or TV stations that run the ads or claims

• interviews with store managers who run questionable ads, sell questionable merchandise, or have questionable store policies

• interviews with product manufacturers that make questionable claims in ads or have shoddy products

• interviews with state or local consumer affairs officials

- interviews with consumers who've shopped at an advertised store or used an advertised product and have personal knowledge of whether claims are true or false

- library research on the particular product, store, or advertising practice

Step B Solve the following puzzle that challenges the math skills of consumers.

Let's say that the normal markup (increase in price over the merchant's cost) is 80% on an item whose list price is $78.50.

The merchant is offering the item at $52.00 and claims that this is 10% over his cost. Is the merchant telling the truth? Show all your calculations and explain your conclusion.

_____

_____

_____

_____

_____

Step C Find the percent markup for the following products using the following Web site to find the retail cost. Browse The Gap Online Store!!

 5. The Gap Online Catalog

Item	Factory Cost	Retail Cost	% Mark-up
Men's Pants	$12		
Women's Pants	$10		
Men's Shoes	$30		
Women's Skirts	$19		
Men's Vests	$25		
Women's Dresses	$15		
Men's Outerwear	$22		
Women's Shoes	$25		
Men's Sweaters	$16		
Women's Sweaters	$35		

Step D Prepare your final report to include:

• an explanation of the ad, claim, or policy that you've questioned and researched, including an explanation of why you questioned it

• what a representative of the newspaper, broadcaster, ad agency, product maker, or store said when confronted with the problem

• the results of your research and analysis that explain whether or not there's a legal or ethical problem with the ad, claim, or policy

• what a consumer can or should do if he or she encounters the problem researched

SHIP IT!

Overview

In this lesson students will analyze maps and cost data to create the most economical flight plan for a cargo jet that must stop at nine United States cities.

Time Frame

Initial Lesson: two 45-minute periods
Extensions: two 45-minute periods

Objectives

- Analyze cost data
- File a flight plan for a cargo jet
- Solve distance and rate problems
- Calculate most efficient solution to a problem

Materials

- Graphing software or spreadsheet (optional)

 # Procedure

1 Have students discuss the cost factors involved in shipping goods by air and identify the variables. These include volume and weight of each package, cost of jet fuel, number of takeoffs and landings, and distances between takeoffs and landings. After listing the variables on the chalkboard, discuss how each affects cost.

2 Have students brainstorm methods for controlling costs associated with each variable.
Identify the costs that the operator of the cargo jet service can and cannot control.

3 For an introduction to this lesson have your students go through the Flight Path Lesson at the Plane Math site. Students should find the shortest flight routes from San Francisco to New York.

WEB SITE **1. Flight Path**

WEB SITE **2. Plane Math**

4 Divide the class into groups of three students. Send each group to:

WEB SITE **3. Flightpath New York**

5 Each group should file a flight plan that moves goods in the most efficient way, given the following:

All flights start from New York and must stop at each city.

If the distance of the flight between two cities is less than 800 miles, the cost is $0.10 for each kilogram of goods shipped multiplied by the distance in miles.

If the distance is greater than 800 miles, the price is $0.20 for each kilogram multiplied by the distance in miles.

Each unit to be shipped weighs 5 kilograms. The quantities to be shipped to each city are as follows:

San Francisco – 1000 units
Spokane – 200 units
Dallas – 800 units
Phoenix – 600 units
Minneapolis – 500 units
Memphis – 200 units
Miami – 900 units
Atlanta – 800 units
Pittsburgh – 300 units

6 Based on the flight plan and cost data, have students create a chart that shows the costs for each segment of the journey as well as the total cost.

Extensions

1 Have your students plan to build a central plant from which to ship all units. Their goal would be to find the best location to minimize shipping costs. They would only have choices from the red dot cities located on the following map:

WEB SITE 4. Map of Cities

2 Your students may need to further explore techniques and strategies for solving problems. Once these steps are integrated into their thinking, problem solving can become a search for patterns in problems. Guide your students through the problems at this site.

WEB SITE 5. 21st Century Problem Solving

3 To alter the activity, adjust which city is the starting point and ask each group to start at a different city. Each plant could then ship a different essential part to each city.

SHIP IT!

NAME: _____

CLASS: _____ DATE:_____

Step A You're in charge of finding the most efficient way to ship goods for your company. Begin by performing the Flight Path Lesson at the Plane Math site on the Internet. You'll be finding the shortest distance via flight routes from San Francisco to New York. This site will take you step by step to each city, letting you choose the flight path and determine the shortest total trip.

WEB SITE 1. Flight Path

WEB SITE 2. Plane Math

Go to the Flight Path New York page.

WEB SITE 3. Flight Path New York

Step B Get together with two classmates. Your task will be to produce a flight plan to move goods in the most efficient way. You will be using the plane routes established from the previous exercise. In doing so, you must consider the following:

All flights start from New York and must stop at each city along the designated flight paths.

If the distance of the flight between two cities is less than 800 miles, the cost is $0.10 for each kilogram of goods shipped multiplied by the distance in miles.

If the distance is greater than 800 miles, the price is $0.20 for each kilogram multiplied by the distance in miles.

Each unit to be shipped weighs 5 kilograms. The quantities to be shipped to each city are as follows:

San Francisco – 1000 units
Spokane – 200 units
Dallas – 800 units
Phoenix – 600 units
Minneapolis – 500 units
Memphis – 200 units
Miami – 900 units
Atlanta – 800 units
Pittsburgh – 300 units

Step C Make two bar graphs that display:

Distance from New York to each city in your flight plan; and total distance.

Costs for each segment from New York to each city in your flight plan; and total cost.

San Francisco																		
Spokane																		
Dallas																		
Phoenix																		
Minneapolis																		
Memphis																		
Miami																		
Atlanta																		
Pittsburgh																		
Total																		

Distance - kilometers

San Francisco																			
Spokane																			
Dallas																			
Phoenix																			
Minneapolis																			
Memphis																			
Miami																			
Atlanta																			
Pittsburgh																			
Total																			

Cost - dollars

BALANCING THE BUDGET

 ## Overview

Balancing the budget is one of the federal government's greatest economic and political concerns. On a much smaller scale, the harmony and well-being of families have also risen and fallen over the issue of personal budgets. In this lesson students analyze the elements of a budget and create a simulated national budget. By doing so, they will gain an appreciation of the importance of budgets in their personal lives.

 ## Time Frame

Initial Lesson: two 45-minute periods
Extensions: two 45-minute periods

 ## Objectives

- Analyze a budget based on federal spending
- Create an effective budget
- Realize possible outcomes from changing budget allowances

Materials

- Computer with Internet access

# Procedure

1 To achieve necessary goals in any economic system, budgeting is required when money is limited. Tell students that they will propose their own simulated budget on a national level using national spending categories. After logging on to the site below, ask them to read the instructions carefully and choose one of the two sites to run their budget simulation. Note: The monetary figures are not provided until after students propose their budget. So students will not at first know how much of the total expenditure each category makes up:

WEB SITE 1. CCER National Budget Simulation

2 Have students break into teams and play the short version of the simulation. Make sure students read the hypertext descriptions of the spending categories so they know where their money is going. The groups should independently discuss which categories to change and come to a consensus. Students should keep notes on how they changed the spending on each category and why.

3 Have students submit their proposals and compare and contrast them with the actual financial figures and changes. Have student groups log their new figures on the board and explain what they cut and added. Let your class discuss and vote on the feasibility of each group's national budget choice.

The class should choose what it considers to be the most practical national budget and compare and contrast it to President Clinton's actual budget proposal for 1995. Students can access this site to gather data about the federal budget President Clinton proposed in 1995 by clicking on "Chart the current budget."

⚏ Extensions

1 For more information and background on the federal budget, students should check out the following Web sites! Have your students specifically find factors determining budget spending that they have never heard of before.

WEB SITE **2. A Citizen's Guide to the Federal Budget**

WEB SITE **3. FAQs About the Budget of the U.S. Government**

2 Students can obtain a copy of Sim City Planning, or any of the Sim series simulations by Maxis, for more in-depth practice of budget, city planning, and related topics. You can find information, including teaching tips, at the Maxis WWW site!

WEB SITE **4. Maxis Home Page**

3 Students may wish to run the long version of the budget simulator for a more detailed exploration of budget elements. You can have students independently focus on a single category and its sub-categories. There are many here to choose from. Then the class will reconvene to submit each part of the new budget proposal.

WEB SITE **5. National Budget Simulation: Long Version**

4 Now have your students apply the concepts of budgets and spending to a household. You can give your students a list of expenses and a set monthly income. Vary when bills are due: weekly, monthly, three times a year, and yearly. Instruct them to go to the following Web site to begin their education on the importance of saving money.

WEB SITE **6. HOW and WHY to SAVE MONEY**

BALANCING THE BUDGET

NAME: _____

CLASS: _____ DATE:_____

Step   A   While playing the budget simulation at the following site answer these questions about your choices.

WEB SITE **1. CCER National Budget Simulation**

1. What category did you cut the most? Why?

_____

_____

_____

2. What category did you increase the most? Why?

_____

_____

_____

Step   B   Fill in the data below from your 1st attempt.

Old budget

_____

New budget

_____

Change in deficit

_____

New deficit

Fill in the data below from your 2nd attempt.

Old budget

_____

New budget

_____

Change in deficit

_____

New deficit

_____

Step C Analyze the following and present your answer below.

1. What happens if you cut more dollars than the current deficit?

_____

_____

_____

_____

2. Using the resources linked to this site, completely detail the repercussions of your largest budget cut. Your detailed explanation should include what your cut would do to the national economy, local economies, personal lives of affected people, etc.

_____

_____

_____

_____

_____

_____

_____

_____

Step D Compare the national budget categories with financial categories of a household. Which categories can be roughly associated with each other. Write an essay from the budgeting concepts you have seen that is titled: 10 Ways Household Budgets are Similar to the Federal Budget!

_____

_____

_____

_____

_____

_____

_____

_____

_____

_____

GRAPHING SPORTS STATISTICS

Overview

In this lesson students sharpen their graph-reading skills by gathering data from Internet sites, interpreting the data, and creating graphs to illustrate the statistics.

Time Frame

2 class periods of 45 minutes

Objectives

- Identify the elements of a line graph and create a graph complete with all its elements
- Research sports data on the Internet and create an appropriate scale to allow the data to be shown on a line graph
- Plot sports data on line graphs and interpret information from other line graphs prepared by classmates

Materials

- Graph paper
- Pencils
- Markers or colored pencils

Procedure

1 Review the elements of a line graph with students by drawing a large, blank graph on the board.

Ask volunteers to point out the x- and y-axes, then label them as if the graph were going to show the number of people entering national parks over a 15-year period. Ask another volunteer to come up with an appropriate title for the graph. Review the importance of choosing a scale for the x- and y-axes that will clearly show the data. Let the class decide as a group what would be a good scale if 132 million people had visited the parks.

2 Explain to students that they'll gather sports data on the Internet and show that data on a graph. Have students go to the ESPN Sportszone to find the performance history of the Dallas Cowboys.

WEB SITE **1. ESPN Sportszone: Dallas Cowboys Historical Performance**

Ask students to note the broken-line graph on the Web page and explain that this is the kind of graph students will create. Have them scroll down to the regular-season statistics for 1980–1989. Explain that they will use data from the first column, team wins, to create their graphs.

3 Label the x- and y-axes "years" and "team wins" respectively, then determine the scale of each axis and label it. Allow time for students to plot their data and connect the dots to complete their graphs. Then have students access the Activity Sheet and answer the questions relating to the graphs they've just created.

4 Next invite students to create another graph, using historical performance statistics of their own favorite teams, other than the Dallas Cowboys. Stress that students can get to other teams' statistics from the list on the left side of the Dallas page. This second graph may be another line graph, or it may be a colorful bar graph, picture graph, or area graph.

Remind students to return to the Activity Sheet to answer any questions about their second graphs.

⛭ Extensions

❶ The following site will give students additional data from which to construct different kinds of sports-statistics graphs. Assign your students to create five graphs each using different statistics.

[WEB SITE] 2. Excite: Home Page

SPORTQuest is another good site for sports stats.

[WEB SITE] 3. SPORTQuest

❷ Suggest that students surf the Web for more sports stats specifying particular sports. Students can use Olympic statistics to make area graphs showing the overall percentage of gold medals won by different nations. The following site has medal breakdowns from past Olympics by events and years.

[WEB SITE] 4. Olympic Statistics

❸ Give students an opportunity to read and interpret graphs. Explain that each week news magazines use graphs to show readers important statistics related to the stories in the magazine. Then, have students open this site to compare graphs.

[WEB SITE] 5. Time Poll Archive

GRAPHING SPORTS STATISTICS

NAME: _____

CLASS: _____ DATE:_____

Step A Today you're going to create some graphs. To gather the data for the first graph—a line graph—sprint over to this site!

(WEB SITE) 1. ESPN Sportszone: Dallas Cowboys Historical Performance

Answer these questions, using the data on the graph you made showing Dallas Cowboys' wins.

In which year did the Cowboys have the most wins?

_____

In which year did the Cowboys have the fewest wins?

_____

How many wins did the Cowboys have in 1987?

_____

Were there more wins in 1982 or 1988?

_____

Does the graph show any trends?

_____

Step B Make a graph about your favorite team, other than the Dallas Cowboys. Follow the links provided on the Dallas page. When your graph is finished, answer the following questions using the data for your own favorite team.

In which years did your team have the most wins?

_____

In which year did the team have the fewest wins?

_____

How many wins did they have in 1990?

_____

Were there more wins in 1984 or 1994?

_____

Does the graph show any trends?

_____

Step **C** Now answer these questions about graphs in general.

1. Which shows trends better, a pie graph or a bar graph?

_____

2. What kind of symbol would you use if you created a picture graph to show statistics for your favorite sports team?

_____

3. Use the statistics for the Cowboys and the statistics for your favorite team to create just one graph, comparing the two teams. Which team had more wins in 1989? Which shows a more promising trend?

From the graph on the previous page write five distinct conclusions about the data represented. Two conclusions must be from the overall representation, two must be from specific points on the graph, and the last must be a silly conclusion that may not seem important to studying the graph.

1.

_____

_____

_____

_____

2.

_____

_____

_____

_____

3.

_____

_____

_____

_____

4.

_____

_____

_____

_____

5.

_____

_____

_____

_____

PLAYING THE STOCK MARKET

Overview

In this lesson students become "investors" in the stock market. As such, they analyze stock data and make simulated purchases and sales of stock.

Time Frame

2 class periods of 45-minutes plus 1 month of independent work

Objectives

• Research the way the stock market works in order to find out how to buy and sell stocks
• Analyze stock data in order to determine when to buy and sell certain stocks
• Perform calculations to determine which stock purchases were profitable and which were not

Materials

• Daily information on stock trades and stock prices from newspapers or the Internet
• Forms for recording stock trades

# Procedure

1 Have students work in pairs and go to the following Web sites where they can learn about the stock market, determine how to buy and sell stocks, and research stocks they might want to "buy."

WEB SITE **1. Investing for Kids**

This Web site is full of information that will explain the stock market, how to trade stocks, how to track them daily, and how to research companies whose stocks students might want to "buy."
To start, have students click on Beginner on the home page and browse through the voluminous information and links.

WEB SITE **2. Good News Bears**

On the home page, students can click on Student Resources to access the Student Resources page.
Click on Tips on Choosing a Stock for links to a number of Web sites that can give students useful information on various stocks they might "buy."

2 Each student pair begins with $10,000. Over a period of one month, students may trade any stocks any number of times. Students should keep records of the following: date of transaction, name of stock purchased or sold, number of shares purchased or sold, price of shares purchased or sold, total investment or receipts. Students should also keep a running total of profits and losses and note the reasons for buying or selling each stock.
They can track their stocks daily using the business pages in a newspaper or Web sites where stock prices are recorded.

WEB SITE **3. Stock Smart**

WEB SITE **4. Fast Quote**

WEB SITE **5. Yahoo! Finance**

3 At the end of a month, students should tally their profits and losses and assess how well they did in the stock market.

4 Have each team report on the results of their month-long investments in the stock market. List profits and losses on the chalkboard. Focus on the top three winners and top three losers and lead a class discussion that analyzes these successes and failures. During the discussion, the teams singled out should defend their positions.

Extensions

1 If students liked this stock trading simulation, they can find others on the Web where they can buy and sell stocks and compare their results to those of other students around the country. Students should start with the following site and create their own portfolio.

WEB SITE **6. Your Portfolio**

2 Students should research the background of companies they'd like to invest in during this simulation. Many large companies have Web sites on the Internet with company profiles and other information of interest to potential investors. Using a search engine for entry to the Net, students should type in the name of the company that is of interest to them.

WEB SITE **7. Yahoo!**

3 If students are interested in daily business news, a number of business publications are online. So are business services of many broadcast and cable news organizations. With the right computer capabilities, students can even hear news reports over the sound system of their computers. Students can use the name of the publication or news organization as a key to access a particular site.

WEB SITE **8. National Public Radio**

PLAYING THE STOCK MARKET

NAME: _____

CLASS: _____ DATE:_____

Step   A   Work in pairs and go to the following Web sites where you can learn about the stock market, how to buy and sell stocks, and research stocks you might want to "buy."

WEB SITE **1. Investing for Kids**

This Web site is filled with information that will explain the stock market, how to buy and sell stocks, how to track them daily, and how to research companies whose stocks you might want to "buy." To start, click on Beginner on the home page and browse through the voluminous information and links.

Pretend you have $10,000 to invest. First, you need to investigate where to invest it. For the following types of investments calculate a maximum estimated annual return from the Beginner tutorial at the Investing for Kids Web site. Also rate the amount of risk for each investment on a scale from 1 to 10.

Type of Investment	Estimated Return	Risk Rating
Bank Accounts		
Bonds		
Stocks		
Other:		

On the home page of the following site, click on Student Resources to access the Student Resources page.

🌐 2. Good News Bears

Click on Tips on Choosing a Stock for links to a number of Web sites that can give you useful information on various stocks you might want to "buy." From the tips given at this site, choose the five most important ones for your personal investing strategy. Write them below.

1.

_____

_____

_____

2.

_____

_____

_____

3.

_____

_____

_____

4.

_____

_____

_____

5.

_____

_____

_____

You will begin with $10,000. Over a period of one month, you may buy and sell any stocks any number of times.

You should keep records of the following: date of transaction, name of stock purchased or sold, number of shares purchased or sold, price of shares purchased or sold, total investment or receipts, profit or loss.

You should keep a running total of profits and losses.

You should note the reasons for buying or selling each stock.

You can track your stocks daily using the business pages in a newspaper or Web sites where stock prices are recorded.

WEB SITE **3. Stock Smart**

WEB SITE **4. Fast Quote**

WEB SITE **5. Yahoo! Finance**

At the end of a month, you should tally your profits and losses and assess how well you did in the stock market.

Advanced
Mathematics

THE KINEMATICS OF ROLLER COASTERS

Overview

It's not hard to see the importance of mathematics to engineers who design roller coasters. Engineers consider many variables in order to design safe and adventurous rides. In this lesson, students will use algebra to analyze America's most thrilling and famous amusement park attractions.

Time Frame

Initial Lesson: one to two 45-minute periods or equivalent
Extensions: 2-5 periods

Objectives

•Differentiate between different variables
•Use algebra to solve problems
•Relate mathematics to physics and engineering

Materials

•Calculators
•Stop watches
•Accelerometers
•50-m tape measure or surveying equipment

# Procedure

1 Discuss roller coasters with students. They will certainly want to reflect upon experiences they've had. Let them lead the discussion with their stories, and then help them identify the most important variables in roller coaster design and operation:

- distance (horizontal and vertical)
- speed
- acceleration
- force
- gravity
- friction

2 Go to this site and browse the information provided for roller coaster fanatics:

WEB SITE **1. Rollercoaster!**

In particular, read the following page and have students identify as many variables as possible (e.g., height, angle, speed...).

WEB SITE **2. The Need For Speed**

3 Teach these kinematics variables and formulas to students. They may already know them from their studies in science. Possibly they encountered the formulas with slightly different symbols than presented here; adjust your presentation accordingly:

VARIABLES
d = distance (h = height)
v = velocity (speed) v_i = initial velocity v_f = final velocity
a = acceleration
g = gravitational acceleration on earth = 9.8 m/s^2 (Students can round to 10.)
m = mass
P.E. = potential energy   K.E. = kinetic energy

UNIT CONVERSIONS
To solve question B-1: 1m = 3.2808 ft., or 1 ft. = 0.3048 m.
To solve question B-2: 1 mi. = 1.609344 km, or 1 km = 0.62137 mi.

FORMULAS

P.E. = mgh

K.E. = $^1/_2mv^2$

V = d/t

a = $(v_f - v_i)/t$

⚙ Extensions

1 Visit the description of these roller coasters at this site and analyze their specifications:

WEB SITE **3. New Coasters '96**

2 Build model amusement park rides with your students. These make great science fair projects. Use common materials such as balsa wood, wire, glue, toys, etc. Students should use their new knowledge of the dynamics of motion along with data collected on the safety tolerances of the ride.

3 Physics Day! In conjunction with high schools across the country, Six Flags hosts thousands of students each year to study elements of physics while they enjoy their favorite rides. You can bring accelerometers, stop watches, and measuring tapes to study the rides there. Contact individual theme parks for school group information and activity kits.

WEB SITE **4. Six Flags Theme Parks**

THE KINEMATICS OF ROLLER COASTERS

NAME: _____

CLASS: _____ DATE: _____

Step   A   Go to the following site to gather information for answering the questions in the next step. You should look for the quantities that determine how exciting the ride is. Your teacher has discussed with you some of these attributes, such as height, acceleration, and velocity. List the data in the space provided below. Be sure to include the description and the units for each number provided.

WEB SITE **5. Superman The Escape**

_____

_____

_____

_____

_____

_____

_____

_____

Step B Answer the following questions, based upon the data you have gathered in Step A. Show all calculations you perform in each question. Start with the formulas your teacher has provided for you at the beginning of the lesson, plug in the variables, show all steps, and give your final answer. Maintain units through your calculations to the best of your ability.

1. If a student has a mass of 40 kg, what is her gravitational potential energy at the peak of the ride?

2. What is the maximum acceleration of the ride?

3. How much would your speed change if you experienced the maximum g-force for three seconds?

4. If the ride moves at an average speed of 20 ft/s, how long would it take to complete the course?

Step C Choose one of the images of the roller coasters pictured at this site. Choose one that looks the coolest to ride on. You will be analyzing the curves of the track for specific points where the forces of motion are in full action.

2. Need For Speed

On the following, a simple sketch of the roller coaster you chose. Label the following critical points along the roller coaster track:

a) A place where the roller coaster will accelerate (gain speed).
b) A place where the roller coaster will decelerate (lose speed).
c) A place where potential energy of the roller coaster is high and kinetic energy is low.
d) A place where kinetic energy of the roller coaster is high and potential energy is low.

My Roller Coaster Sketch

THE MATHEMATICS OF MUSIC

Overview

Music and mathematics are closely intertwined. The pitch of a musical note is determined by the frequency, or vibrations per second, of the sound waves emanating from the instrument. The volume is determined by the amplitude (size) of the waves. Understanding the relation of harmonic and discordant notes requires a study of their relative frequencies.

Time Frame

Initial Lesson: one 45-minute period or equivalent.
Extensions: 2 periods.

Objectives

•Quantify variables associated with music and sound.
•Use algebra to analyze musical relations.

Materials

•Calculator
•Tuning Forks (or piano)
•Musical Instruments
•OPTIONAL: Oscilloscope interfaced with microphone; or multi-media computer with sound-editing software.

# Procedure

1 Using the tuning forks, give students a lesson in musical pitch. To sound a tuning fork, bang it against a rubber mat or the sole of your shoe, and place the base firmly on a table or sound box. If the frequency of two notes is a 2 to 1 ratio, the notes are an octave apart. For instance, C-512 is one octave higher than C-256. Notes whose frequencies are in simple whole number ratios sound pleasing when played together and are said to be harmonious. For instance, G-384 and C-256 are in a 3:2 ratio; play them together, and see how melodious they appear together. Notes whose frequencies are not in simple, whole number ratios sound discordant together. Composers and musicians know this and use such knowledge in their craft.

2 Go to this site to learn more about the algebra of acoustics:

WEB SITE 1. Pianos and Continued Fractions

Note how simple, whole number ratios prevail in musical structure.

RATIO	MUSICAL "TONIC"
2:1	octave
3:2	fifth
4:3	fourth

3 Look for these mathematical functions in the analysis of music at the same site:

•Ratios (fractions)
  Ratios are used to construct a scale by frequency.

•Exponents
  Exponents are used to calculate the repetitive frequency jump up perfect fifths in a scale.

•Logarithms
  Logarithms are used when solving problems involving unknowns in the exponents

•Square roots
Square roots can be used to find the frequency ratio of perfect fifths in a chromatic scale.

Extensions

1 Repeat the activities in step one, using musical instruments brought in by students.

2 Use a computer with a microphone and software such as SoundEdit to analyze the wave forms of various sounds. With such software, you can zoom in on the waves and analyze their relative frequency and amplitude. Waves produced by sounds an octave apart will have a 2:1 ratio in their wavelength, measured from peak to peak.

3 If you want to learn more about the interplay between music and mathematics, you can start your search at this site:

WEB SITE **2. Rhythm & Ratios**

100

THE MATHEMATICS OF MUSIC
....
TEACHING MATHEMATICS WITH THE INTERNET

THE MATHEMATICS OF MUSIC

NAME: _____

CLASS: _____ DATE:_____

Go to this site and complete the steps based upon what you read there:

WEB SITE 1. Pianos and Continued Fractions

Step A Musical intervals such as "octaves" and "fifths" are based upon frequency ratios. Complete the following table:

FREQUENCY RATIO	MUSICAL TERM
3:2	perfect fifth
2:1	
	perfect fourth
5:4	
	minor third

Step B Note the importance of logarithms throughout this site and how calculations are carried out. Solve the following log problems, showing all work. The first is done for you.

1) $\log_2 32 = x$
    $32 = 2^x$
    $x = 5$

(In other words, $\log_a b$ is the exponent to which you would have to raise a to get b.)

2) $\log_2 8$
3) $\log_3 9$
4) $\log_4 64$
5) $\log_5 125$
6) $\log_{16} 4$

Step   C   In a paragraph or two, explain the legend of the Pythagorean Hammers and what it tells us about the composition of Western music.

Briefly recount the legend of the Pythagorean Hammers:

_____

_____

_____

_____

_____

_____

_____

_____

_____

_____

_____

_____

_____

_____

_____

_____

_____

_____

_____

_____

Explain its relevance to Western music:

_____

_____

_____

_____

_____

_____

_____

_____

_____

_____

_____

_____

_____

_____

_____

_____

CHAOS, ORDER & FRACTALS

 ## Overview

Chaos theory may turn out to follow relativity and quantum mechanics as the third great revolution in twentieth-century theoretical physics. An exploding field of mathematics that has enormous scientific implications, it arose rather recently, in the past two decades. Students will gain an introduction to this field through formulas, patterns, and images poised between order and chaos.

 ## Time Frame

Initial Lesson: one 45-minute period or equivalent
Extensions: 1-2 periods

 ## Objectives

- Distinguish between ordered and chaotic patterns
- Generate fractal patterns
- Link mathematics of chaos theory to natural science

 ## Materials

- String
- Spring
- Weight
- Ring stand or other support
- Maps
- Leaves or plants
- Pencil
- Ruler

Procedure

1 Discuss the difference between ordered and chaotic systems. How does a pile of bricks differ from a brick wall? What ordered events and phenomena exist in nature, and what chaotic ones? Hang a weight from a string mounted on a ring stand. Give it a push and watch it swing back and forth. Then replace the string with a spring and note the difference. A spring-based pendulum quickly goes into a disordered type of motion. The behavior of the first pendulum can be analyzed with simple formulas, but the second becomes unpredictable in a short period of time.

2 Read the short tutorial on this page:

WEB SITE **1. The Fractal Microscope**

In particular, note the defining formula of the Mandelbrot set, and the associated images. Features which characterize fractals:

- Mathematical basis: fractals are graphical representations generated by mathematical functions.
- Repetition: Patterns are repeated over and over again, in various ways.
- Self similarity: zooming in on a magnified portion reveals patterns apparent on larger scales.
- Complexity: One reason fractal science is exploding is that the numerous and complex computations required to generate these shapes could only be performed recently, when powerful computers came of age.

3 Note the formulas and methods used to generate fractal-type patterns at these two sites:

WEB SITE **2. The Sierpinski Triangle**

WEB SITE **3. Fibonacci Numbers and Nature**

(Scroll down to The Fibonacci Spiral and examine the successive generation of squares.)

Fractal patterns and chaos theory apply to many natural phenomena:

- •snowflakes
- •coastlines
- •branching of plants
- •population genetics

Computers often employ fractal mathematics to render screen images. What other examples of ordered chaos can your students think of in nature?

Extensions

1 Learn more about the work of Benoit Mandelbrot and Mandelbrot sets at this site:

WEB SITE 4. Julia and Mandelbrot Sets

2 Sets of different fractal image families are visible here:

WEB SITE 5. Fractal Pictures & Animations

3 Play The Chaos Game to generate a Sierpinski triangle using these directions:

WEB SITE 6. The Chaos Game

CHAOS, ORDER & FRACTALS

NAME: _____

CLASS: _____ DATE:_____

Step A Describe the repetition and self-similarity in the images on this page:

WEB SITE **7. Miscellaneous Pictures**

What patterns are repeated? What natural phenomena are suggested?

_____

_____

_____

_____

Step B Draw a Koch Snowflake. It starts with the equilateral triangle at left. Then you erase the middle third of each side and introduce another point, as shown. Repeat for the other two sides. Then do this again for each of the twelve new, smaller sides.

Can you make any conclusions about the perimeter of the fractals you started to draw?

_____

_____

What is happening to the perimeter as you move from the first triangle to the second triangle shape?

_____

_____

What happens as you go further in the drawings?

_____

_____

What would happen to the perimeter if you kept repeating this pattern to infinity?

_____

_____

For more discussion on this phenomenon go to the following Web site.

8. The Koch Snowflake

Step **C** Visit these sites to zoom in on fractals and watch their animated forms:

9. Sprott's Fractal Gallery

10. Fractal Movies

(If you have the capacity to view movies and have a fast Internet connection—the movies are large!)

Step **D** Now, invent a fractal of your own with a partner. Decide upon a mathematical formula or recurring pattern. Explain how it works, describe how it is generated, and sketch a portion:

How it works:

_____

_____

_____

_____

How it is generated:

_____

_____

_____

_____

Sketch:

TRIGONOMETRIC FUNCTIONS

 ## Overview

Trigonometry is a branch of mathematics based upon angles and triangles, with applications throughout science and engineering. In this lesson, students will gain familiarity and practice with the most basic and important trigonometric functions: sine, cosine, and tangent.

 ## Time Frame

Initial Lesson: two 45-minute periods or equivalent
Extensions: 2 periods

Objectives

- Define trigonometric functions, including sine, cosine, and tangent
- Define inverse trigonometric functions
- Relate trigonometry to engineering and science

 ## Materials

- Calculator with trigonometric functions
- SPECIAL BROWSER NEEDS: Java-capable Browser (Netscape 3.0+ or Explorer 3.01+)

 # Procedure

❶ Define the functions sine, cosine, and tangent. This is usually done in reference to the ratio of the legs of a right triangle, or a unit circle superimposed upon a coordinate axis. There is a very good image and associated definitions at this site:

🌐 1. Trigonometric Functions

The mnemonic "SOH CAH TOA" is useful for remembering the definitions.

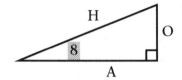

In the triangle pictured, the
   SINE of the angle equals the length of the OPPOSITE side divided by the HYPOTENUSE.
   COSINE of the angle equals the length of the ADJACENT side divided by the HYPOTENUSE.
   TANGENT of the angle equals the length of the OPPOSITE side divided by the ADJACENT side.

Another nice reference page you can start at on the Web:

🌐 2. FAQs about Trigonometry

❷ Another way to visualize sine and cosine functions is the "shadow" cast by a unit-1 circle-radius on the x and y axes of a Cartesian grid:

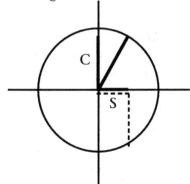

With a Java-capable browser you can view this at these sites:

(WEB SITE) 3. Stick and Shadows (Part 1)

(WEB SITE) 4. Stick and Shadows (Part 2)

❸ Discuss some of the uses for trigonometry:

- •surveying in map making
- •astronomy
- •engineering (i.e., building bridges, buildings)
- •acoustics (sound waves can be analyzed with trigonometric functions)

Explore the history of trigonometry at this site:

(WEB SITE) 5. The Trigonometric Functions

Extensions

❶ Java-capable browsers will show the shape of a sine wave at this site:

(WEB SITE) 6. Sine and Cosine Do "the Wave"

❷ Pronounce "sine" properly by listening in on this site:

(WEB SITE) 7. Sine Pronunciation

❸ For some trigonometric problems on the Internet go to the following sites. The Math Forum has a comprehensive list of math sites dealing in the topic of trigonometry.

(WEB SITE) 8. Vectors & Trigonometry

(WEB SITE) 9. Math Forum Collection: Trigonometry

TRIGONOMETRIC FUNCTIONS

NAME: _____

CLASS: _____ DATE:_____

 Step   A   Go to these sites and answer the questions below based upon your understanding of trigonometry. Show your work:

WEB SITE 1. Trigonometric Functions

WEB SITE 10. Triangles, Circles, and Waves (oh my!): An Overview of Trigonometry

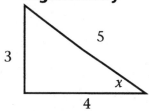

1. What is the sine of angle *x* in the triangle?

2. What is the cosine of angle *x* in the triangle?

3. What is the tangent of angle *x* in the triangle?

4. What is the measure of angle *x* in the triangle? (HINT: Use the inverse functions of your calculator; for instance, the inverse function of sine is arcsine or sine-1.)

Step **C** Use a unit circle and the Pythagorean theorem to prove this trigonometric identity:

$$\sin^2(x) + \cos^2(x) = 1$$

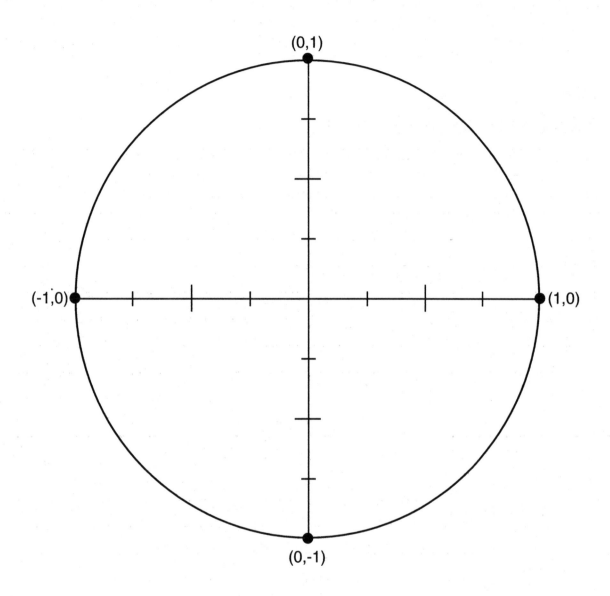

CALCULUS GRAPHICS

 Overview

Calculus is a very visual branch of mathematics. Theoreticians in this field study lines, curves, and solids. In this activity, students will study colorful images depicting lines, curves, solids, and limits.

 Time Frame

Initial Lesson: one 45-minute period or equivalent
Extensions: 3 periods

 Objectives

•Conceptualize limits of points and tangents
•Learn circumscription/inscription method of determining Pi
•Place calculus in a historical context

Materials

•SPECIAL BROWSER NEEDS: MPEG Animation Viewer such as Sparkle
•Graph paper
•Ruler
•Construction paper
•Glue
•Graphing calculator
•Cups (or cylinders) and measuring cups (or beakers)

# Procedure

1 Go to the Calculus Graphics home page and view the images there with students. Lead a discussion with students on how calculus developed as a branch of mathematics and why it's important to us today. The site gives a refreshing look at calculus using animations. It also discusses some early attempts in using limits to solve problems. These were precursors to modern calculus:

1. Graphics for the Calculus Classroom

Archimedes invented calculus in ancient Greece to solve his more difficult "philosophical" problems. Newton refined this complex branch of mathematics in his historic Seventeenth-Century treatise, Principia Mathematica, widely regarded as the most important scientific work ever written.

2 Your students will be analyzing calculus graphics denoting the limit's effects on functions. Look for these important elements in the array of images at the Graphics for the Calculus Classroom site:

- Calculus assigns slopes to infinitesimally small portions of curves by considering the slope of tangent lines.
- Calculus can be used to find the volume of the intersection of two solids.
- Calculus can be used to refine the known value of important mathematical constants such as Pi.
- Calculus can be used to examine the limit of a function as it approaches some value.

3 Scroll down to "Differentials and differences" and have students take turns reading the tutorial there. Then click on the animation.

4 Use a graphing calculator to generate different curves associated with mathematical functions, then zoom in and out to examine the appearance of the graphs at different scales.

⚙ Extensions

❶ Students read the passage "Computing the volume of water in a tipped glass," and study the associated formulas, images, and animations. Then they try to predict theoretical values for a glass of given dimensions, angle, and water level, and compare them to actual, measured values using drinking glasses and water. If cylindrical cups are not available, use jars or cans. Or borrow beakers from the science labs to make volume measurements. Beakers serve a double purpose: their shape is nearly cylindrical, and they are marked with volume increments.

❷ Visit the Famous Curves Index. This Web page is a hyperlink directory of all of the historic curves in mathematics. It provides the historical background of each curve. Most of the discussions center around curves from calculus class.

WEB SITE 2. Famous Curves Index

❸ Have students graph a common curve such as $y = x^2$, and then approximate the area under a portion of that curve by cutting out paper rectangles and filling the region. Assemble as a collage on construction paper and post on your bulletin board.

❹ Use the images at the following Web page to discuss the possible differences in finding the limit of a function at a given point. There are pictures of situations where right-hand and left-hand limits differ or instances where the limit does not exist.

WEB SITE 3. Limits

CALCULUS GRAPHICS

NAME: _____

CLASS: _____ DATE:_____

Step   A   Read the passages "Secants and tangents" and "Zooming in on a tangent line" at this site and view the associated animations. Then answer the questions below.

1. Graphics for the Calculus Classroom

1. Consider the slope of the secant lines converging upon the tangent line in the "Secants and tangents" animation. Describe the numerical slope of the line as it passes through the various states of convergence during the animation.

_____

_____

_____

_____

The slope is given in the animation at the top left corner. How can this scenario be applied to limits? Write a formula for finding the tangent using secants and limits. Show your work.

2. Study the animation "Zooming in on a tangent line." What happens to the apparent shape of the curve as you zoom in?

_____

_____

_____

_____

_____

_____

_____

_____

Step   B   Read the passage on "the limit" at the above site. Then look at the close-up gif image of several graphs:

WEB SITE 3. Limits

Considering the upper left of the four graphs, complete this table of values of the limit of $f(x)$ as x approaches the given values:

x	LIMIT OF $f(x)$
0.0	___
0.5	___
1.0	-5
1.5	___
2.0	___

Step   C   Read the passage on "Archimedes' Calculation of Pi." View the seven associated images. Write a paragraph describing the strategy Archimedes employed to find Pi, and how successful he was.

_____

_____

_____

_____

_____

_____

_____

_____

_____

_____

_____

_____

_____

_____

_____

_____

Step   D   The table at the site listed below shows the value of Pi as determined by Archimedes' method if it was continued beyond the capabilities of Archimedes.

 4. Table of Results

n = number of sides	area of polygon
4	2
6	2.59808
8	2.82843
12	3

The area of a regular polygon inscribed in a unit circle is:

$$n * Sin[180°/n] * Cos[180°/n]$$

From the equation given at the following site set up a limit problem that will simulate what Archimedes was trying to perform. You will need a formula for finding the area of a generic polygon given above. From that formula you can solve for Pi by using limits. Remember you will need to set your limit to go to infinity.

Answer Key

Activity Sheet 1: The Geometry of Visual Perspective

1) The apparent point at which parallel lines intersect in the distance; **2)** similar; **3)** Florence, Italy, 1400's; **4)** rectangle; **5)** trapezoid; **6)** e.g., AB and DC, the top and bottom edges of the window; **7)** they are parallel; **8)** any window corner, e.g., BC and DC.

Activity Sheet 2: Tessellations & Eschers

STEP A:

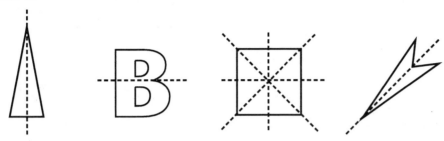

STEP B: triangles (3), squares (4), hexagons (6).
STEP C: Answers will vary.
STEP D: Penrose's tiling system is non-repeating. There is no way you can rotate and/or shift the infinite pattern so that the rotated/shifted pattern is the same as the original pattern. To put it another way, aperiodic tiling lacks symmetry.

Activity Sheet 3: The Pythagorean Theorem

STEP A: **1)** 15; **2)** 30; **3)** 26; **4)** 2.

Activity Sheet 4: Polygons and Polyhedra

STEP A:

NAME	INTERIOR SIDES	ANGLE	EXAMPLE
triangle	3	60	side of tent
square	4	90	side of box
pentagon	5	108	U.S. military headquarters
hexagon	6	120	bathroom tiles
octagon	8	135	some clocks

STEP B: square, 36 sq. cm; triangle, 60 sq. cm; rectangle, 72 sq. cm; trapezoid, 72 sq. cm.
STEP C: Students can identify hexagons in carbon benzene rings; multiple-sided polyhedra in buckminsterfullerenes (e.g., C60); pyramids, tetragons, and other structures.

Activity Sheet 5: Mathematics and Molecules

STEP A:

NAME	# OF CARBONS	# OF TOTAL ATOMS
methane	1	5
ethane	2	8
propane	3	11
butane	4	14
pentane	5	17
hexane	6	20
septane	7	23
octane	8	26

STEP B: f(n) = 3n+2

STEP C: e.g., carbon atoms tend to have four bonds at 109° angles (tetrahedral) when singly bonded; water bonds at 105˚; water forms a hexagonal structure when it freezes into ice; hexagons have 120° angles.

Activity Sheet 6: Pi π
STEP A:

1)

DATE	# OF DECIMAL PLACES
500 BC	0 places
800 AD	4 places
1600 AD	35 places
1990 AD	2 billion

2) e.g., Bible gave Pi=3; Egyptian/Mesopotamian Pi=square root of ten=3.162.
3) 22/7, 223/71, 355/113.

STEP B:

CIRCLE RADIUS	DIAMETER	CIRCUMFERENCE	AREA
1 cm	2 cm	6.28 cm	3.14 cm^2
3	6	18.84	28.26
5	10	31.4	78.5
10	20	62.8	314

STEP C: **1)** a.108 b.36 c.432, it increases four times d.72, it doubles **2)** a.113.097 b.37.6991 c.452.39, it increases four times d.75.3982, it doubles **3)** The concepts stay the same. The theory behind circles and the use of pi does not change. Just the measurements change.

Activity Sheet 7: Fibonacci Sequences
1) 28, 32, $f(n)=4n$; **2)** 243, 729, $f(n)=3^n$; **3)** 49, 64, $f(n)=x^2$; **4)** e.g., the limit of $f(n+1)/f(n)$ as n approaches infinity; **5)** 40, 104, 273...; STEP C) e.g., bees, shells, sneezwort branches, flower petals, plant leaves.

Activity Sheet 8: Logic & Games
STEPS A & B: **1)** valid; **2)** invalid; **3)** valid; **4)** invalid; **5)** invalid; **6)** valid; **7)** Modus Tollens (Denying the Consequent); **8)** Modus Ponens (Affirming the Antecedent); **9)** Denying the Antecedent; **10)** Affirming the Consequent.

STEP C: i.e., first two should be true; second two may be false (are not necessarily true).
STEP D: Answers provided at the Web site of the activity sheet.

Activity Sheet 9: Prime Numbers
STEP A:
24: 2, 3, 4, 6, 8, 12
35: 5, 7
50: 2, 5, 10, 25
8: 2, 4

STEP B: **1)** A perfect number is one whose proper divisors sum to the number itself. e.g. 6, 28; **2)** There is an infinite number of primes; **3)** Every integer can be written as a product of primes in an essentially unique way; **4)** Fermat; **5)** false; **6)** e.g., The Twin Primes Conjecture that there are infinitely many pairs of primes only 2 apart.

STEP C: 1, 3, 7, 31, 127.

Activity Sheet 10: Virtual Dice

STEP A:

DIE A	1	2	3	4	5	6
DIE B						
1	2	3	4	5	6	7
2	3	4	5	6	7	8
3	4	5	6	7	8	9
4	5	6	7	8	9	10
5	6	7	8	9	10	11
6	7	8	9	10	11	12

STEP B:

DICE	TOTAL NUMBER OF APPEARANCES
2	1
3	2
4	3
5	4
6	5
7	6
8	5
9	4
10	3
11	2
12	1

STEP C: **1)** 7 appears the most frequently; **2)** 2 ("snake eyes") and 12 ("box-cars") have the lowest frequency; **3)** one in $2^3 = 8$; **4)** one in four; **5)** one in thirteen; **6)** one in fifty-two.

Activity Sheet 11: Customer Cents
STEP B: Merchant's cost is $43.61; 10% over Merchant's cost is $47.97; No, the merchant is not telling the truth. $52 is a 19% markup from $43.61.

STEP C: Cost and Percent Markup will vary depending on the prices at the Web site.

Activity Sheet 12: Ship It!
Shipping plans will vary. Do not assess how much money the students save, but the problem solving strategies they employ.

Activity Sheet 13: Balancing the Budget
STEP C: The country could fall into a recession.

Activity Sheet 14: Sports Statistics
STEP A: **1)** 1992; **2)** 1989; **3)** 7; **4)** 1982; **5)** Steady success during 60's and 70's, then erratic.

STEP B: Answers will vary depending on the team they choose.
STEP C: Bar chart, football.

Activity Sheet 15: Playing the Stock Market
Estimated returns, ~5%,~10%,~15%. The rest of answers will vary.

Activity Sheet 16: The Kinematics of Roller Coasters

STEP A: Breakthrough Ride Features:
•Speed--100 mph
•Height--415-feet (taller than the landmark Sky Tower)
•Acceleration--0-100 mph in 7 seconds
•Weightlessness--6.5 seconds
•Gravity Forces--4.5 G's
•Total Track Length--1,235-feet
•Capacity--1,800 riders per hour

STEP B: **1)** Use PE=mgh to get 49,585 joules (kgm^2/s^2). **2)** Use $a = (v_f - v_i)/t$ to get 44.7 m/s^2. **3)** Use $a = (v_f - v_i)/t$, with a = (4.5) (9.8m/s^2), v_i = 0, and t = 3 sec, to get v_f = 132.3 m/s. **4)** Use $v = d/t$ to get 62 seconds.

Activity Sheet 17: The Mathematics of Music
STEP A:

FREQUENCY RATIO	MUSICAL TERM
3:2	perfect fifth
2:1	octave
4:3	perfect fourth
5:4	major third
6:5	minor third

STEP B: **2)** 3; **3)** 2; **4)** 3; **5)** 3; **6)** 0.5 or $^1/_2$
STEP C: Answers may vary.

Activity Sheet 18: Chaos, Order, & Fractals
Step A: Students should identify some repetition; natural analogues might include coastlines, atmosphere, cells, etc.

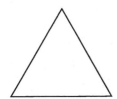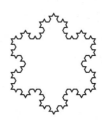

STEP B: The perimeter increased from the first fractal to the second. The perimeter increases for every iteration even though it may be small. It gets very hard to track or calculate the perimeter, but it makes sense that it still increases. You would get infinite perimeter.

STEP C: Fractals will vary.

Activity Sheet 19: Trigonometric Functions
STEP A: **1)** 0.6; **2)** 0.8; **3)** 0.75; **4)** 36.9 degrees;
STEP B: see sine graphs at these sites:

Trigonometry
URL: http://www2.ncsu.edu/unity/lockers/users/f/felder/public/
    kenny/papers/trig.html

Sketchpad 3.0 GalleryURL:
http://forum.swarthmore.edu/sketchpad/gsp.gallery/algebra/algebra.html

STEP C: Students should draw a unit circle imposed upon a set of coordinate axes:

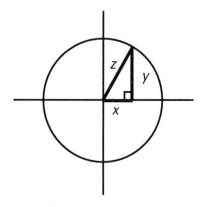

Proof based upon the following correspondences:
    y is the sine of the angle
    x is the cosine of the angle
    z is the radius of the unit circle = 1

Activity Sheet 20: Calculus Graphics
STEP A: **1)** The slope is negative at first. It increases to zero when the line is horizontal. It continues to increase to a positive value; $\tan(x) = \lim (f(x_1) - f(x_2))/(x_1 - x_2)$ **2)** The curve more nearly approximates the tangent line in its shape. The closer you zoom in, the more it appears linear:

STEP B:

X	LIMIT OF f(x)
0.0	2
0.5	0
1.0	-5
1.5	-13
2.0	2

STEP C: Answers will vary.
STEP D: $\lim (n * \mathrm{Sin}[180°/n] * \mathrm{Cos}[180°/n])$